The United States continues to face a complex security environment marked by a broad spectrum of dissimilar threats emerging from countries and highly adaptive transnational terrorist networks. DIA is focused on immediate and long-term threats to allied forces in Afghanistan; risks posed by transnational terrorist organizations, especially as they relate to threats to military forces and facilities; the threat of weapons of mass destruction falling into the hands of non-state actors and the proliferation of these weapons to state actors; monitoring the potential threat to the U.S. from ongoing conflicts; the emergence of foreign militaries with near peer capabilities; and support for US and Allied forces, at sea or on the ground, deployed around the world.

Defense intelligence must be able to provide timely and actionable intelligence across the entire threat spectrum. Our assessments are based upon the agency's worldwide human intelligence, technical intelligence, counterintelligence, and document and media exploitation capabilities, along with information from DIA's partners in the IC and the entire defense intelligence enterprise, international allies, and open sources. In cooperation with these partners and allies, DIA is strengthening its collection and analysis as well as sharing more information across intelligence disciplines, and with our nation's close allies, to better understand the multitude of the threats facing the nation.

The men and women of DIA know they have a unique responsibility to the American people and take great pride in their work. I am privileged to serve with them and present their analysis to you. On behalf of the entire defense intelligence enterprise, thank you for your continuing confidence. Your support is vital to us.

I will begin my testimony first with an assessment of Afghanistan, where the Department of Defense (DoD), the IC, DIA, and our coalition partners remain actively engaged supporting military operations against the threat of al-Qa'ida and other anti-government of Afghanistan forces, transition to global threats, and conclude with an overview of other regional challenges.

# AFGHANISTAN

As the International Security Assistance Force (ISAF) continues the transition in Afghanistan, the Afghan government and the Afghan National Security Forces (ANSF) will seek to conduct presidential and provincial council elections in 2014 and maintain security following the ANSF's assumption of full security responsibilities lead for all of Afghanistan in 2013.

Afghan Security Forces have shown progress in their ability to clear insurgents from contested areas, but have exhibited problems holding cleared areas long-term.   As an auxiliary to Afghanistan's formal security forces, the Afghan Local Police (ALP) continued to support broader efforts by securing some rural areas that might otherwise lack a central government presence.

Operationally, Afghan forces have adapted to the reduction of ISAF enabler support by making better use of their own capabilities and showing tactical competence in planning and conducting security operations.  However, they struggle due to the lack of intelligence, surveillance and reconnaissance, (ISR) capability, as well as expertise in, and technology for countering counter-improvised explosive device (IED) programs. This challenge, along with stretched ANSF airlift and logistical capacity, limits the Afghan National Army's (ANA) ability to sustain operations outside of large urban areas and logistical hubs.  They have been unable to deny freedom of movement to the insurgency in rural areas.

Uncertainty over the post-2014 security environment – U.S. presence, funding, government cohesion and Taliban strength – is likely to drive decisions at all levels over the next year as ANSF leaders are forced to prioritize objectives, while hedging against this uncertainty. Influential power brokers and regional security officials are increasingly concerned with strengthening their influence over ANSF units and ensuring security across their respective areas of authority. These competing priorities could result in politically driven missions that undermine the ANSF's ability to address militarily necessary requirements.

The Afghan National Army (ANA) and Afghan National Police (ANP) manning of approximately 340,000 personnel remained short of the funded ceiling of 352,000. High attrition, low recruitment, and inconsistent pay reduce the ANA's on-hand strength and remain an impediment to the ANA's resilience.

The number of insider attacks from within the Afghan security forces against ISAF personnel significantly decreased in 2013 (13 incidents compared to 48 in 2012). This change is likely a result of a reduced ISAF presence and improved mitigation efforts by both ISAF and the ANSF. The number of insider attacks against Afghan security force personnel increased to 76 incidents, compared to 50 in 2012. Approximately half of all attacks involved ANP as perpetrators, and the ALP accounted for the second largest share.

Afghanistan's political stability depends on successful elections in 2014 and the subsequent transfer of power from President Hamid Karzai to his successor. Afghan preparations for the April 5th presidential and provincial council elections are on track. The lack of a consensus candidate could lead to a potentially destabilizing runoff election that would occur during the peak of the insurgent fighting season and ISAF's drawdown. Post-election stability will depend on the new president's ability to maintain the support of the political elite and ANSF through balanced allocation of political positions and domestic and international funding.

President Karzai remains resistant to signing the Afghan-U.S. Bilateral Security Agreement (BSA) despite the approval of the November 2013 Loya Jirga and popular support, most recently insisting that pre-conditions concerning the Afghan peace process and raids on Afghan homes be met. The delay in signing the BSA increases the risk to political cohesion as the potential loss of foreign assistance prompts Afghan elites to reevaluate the viability of, and support for, the government.

Persistent human capital shortages, weak institutions, and corruption will continue to limit the reach of the central government, impede service delivery, and erode the government's connection to the population. Powerbrokers will strengthen their patronage networks in anticipation of an uncertain future post-2014, encouraging devolution of power.

In 2013, the Taliban-led insurgency failed to seize and hold territory in two of its traditional strongholds, Kandahar and Helmand Provinces. However, we assess the insurgency was able to sustain nationwide violence levels comparable to those of the past two years, with attacks increasingly directed against ANSF. Taliban senior leaders likely believe that they only need to continue present levels of military engagement to be postured for victory following ISAF drawdown and withdrawal of key ANSF enablers. The Haqqani Network is a semiautonomous organization under the broader Taliban insurgency, which we judge to be the most proficient group planning and conducting spectacular and complex attacks in Afghanistan. The Haqqani Network poses a serious and ongoing threat to U.S. personnel and facilities in Afghanistan.

The Taliban maintains public opposition to any negotiations with the Afghan government and further intends to challenge its legitimacy by impeding the presidential election scheduled for April 2014, using violence and intimidation to deter prospective voters and disrupt the process. The Taliban is also making proactive efforts to build political legitimacy in advance of ISAF's drawdown, increasingly attempting to provide limited civil services to local populations. Reduced Coalition presence will present new opportunities for the Taliban to mobilize local sentiment and increase their political influence in the rural areas, their main constituency. We judge Taliban leaders will likely be challenged to fulfill governance roles at the national level or in major urban centers with any degree of competency in the near term. Bottom line, the Taliban offer no more than an economic and social dead end.

Regarding Iranian influence in Afghanistan, Iran maintains a moderate degree of economic leverage over Afghanistan, which it has attempted to use to extract political concessions from the Afghan government with limited success. Iran is a key trade partner, providing critical imports of fuel to Afghanistan. Iran also hosts approximately three million Afghan refugees and, in May of last year, threatened their expulsion if the Afghan parliament approved the U.S.-Afghan Strategic Partnership Agreement. Although the threat was unsuccessful in deterring the agreement, a mass deportation from Iran would cause a humanitarian crisis inside Afghanistan.

Al-Qa'ida leaders continue to view participation in attacks against the Coalition as central to their standing as leader of the global jihad. Despite the outflow of fighters to Syria, the historical and symbolic importance of Afghanistan remains. A small Al-Qa'ida presence resides in the northeastern mountains, with pockets of its fighters elsewhere in the country; however, the group's operational capacity in Afghanistan is limited. We expect al-Qa'ida to use media statements to hail the pending 2014 drawdown as a victory for jihadists, and continue its limited support to the Afghan insurgency.

## GLOBAL THREATS

### CYBER

Cyber reconnaissance, exploitation, and the potential for attacks against DoD forces around the globe is a reality. These activities indicate an interest in how DOD operates in cyberspace and may allow our adversaries to identify opportunities to try to disrupt or degrade military operations. Additionally, state actors are using cyber espionage in attempts to steal critical information from DoD and defense contractors. We remain concerned about this persistent threat to our ability to plan, prepare and ready our forces for future conflicts.

The U.S., the DoD, and our interdependent defense systems and critical infrastructure continue to rely on the convergence of military networks and the Internet to enable us to perform our mission. As other nations develop military cyber warfare doctrine and cyber forces, we know they will cultivate tactics, techniques, tools, capabilities, and procedures to threaten our technological superiority. It is imperative that we understand the adversaries' intent and capabilities.

As conflict between states evolves, the cyberspace is becoming an increasingly vital component of strategy and doctrine for war fighting. Non-state actors remain unpredictable, and the entry barrier to procure disruptive cyber tools and capabilities remains very low. We need to be vigilant to the broader set of state and non-state actors that continue to see cyber as a domain for offensive and defensive influence and opportunity. DoD must strengthen our understanding of the complexities of our adversaries, protect our systems, build resilience in our critical infrastructure, and leverage the experience and knowledge of our foreign partners.

The role the Internet and communication networks play in political stability and regime change remains a significant global cyber issue. Repressive governments are attempting to assert their control over information transmitted through cyberspace, and several nations advocate policies to centralize control over the internet though a top-down intergovernmental approach. Not only would such proposals slow the pace of innovation and hamper global economic development, they would undermine the current, successful multi-stakeholder approach to Internet governance and frustrate the interoperability of networks upon which DoD relies.

## COUNTERINTELLIGENCE

Globalization, rapid technological advancements, and an uncertain fiscal environment present new avenues of collection and threats from traditional nation-state intelligence services and non-state entities to target U.S. national security information, systems, and personnel. Increased financial pressures due to resource cuts create potential vulnerabilities that foreign intelligence entities seek to exploit to identify vulnerable employees and contractors with access to sensitive and classified national security information. Foreign intelligence entities conduct a wide range of intelligence and clandestine activities that threaten and undermine our national security interests and objectives worldwide. Such actors target our armed forces; our military and national security-related research, development, and acquisition activities; our national intelligence system; and our government's decision making processes. In addition to threats by foreign intelligence entities, insider threats will also pose a persistent challenge. Trusted insiders with the intent to do harm can exploit their access to compromise vast amounts of sensitive and classified information as part of personal ideology or at the direction of a foreign government. The unauthorized disclosure of this information to state adversaries, non-state activists, or other entities will continue to pose a critical threat.

DIA is leading an Information Review Task Force to examine grave damage caused to Department of Defense equities and US national security as a result of the unauthorized NSA disclosures. An emerging threat that concerns the department involves the potential for foreign intelligence entities to compromise critical supply chains or corrupt key components bound for vital war-fighting systems. Additionally, a few transnational terrorist groups have developed effective intelligence and counterintelligence capabilities—we have seen this manifest in Iraq and Afghanistan, and terrorist groups are now using and sharing the knowledge and experience they gained in those conflicts.

## TRANSNATIONAL TERRORIST THREATS

**Al-Qa'ida Command and Control:** Several years of sustained counterterrorism pressure have degraded al-Qa'ida's Pakistan-based leadership. Al-Qa'ida is now forced to rely on a limited cadre of experienced leaders, who are restricted to operating primarily inside a Haqqani Network-facilitated safehaven in North Waziristan, Pakistan. This pressure has made it difficult for al-Qa'ida to replenish its senior ranks with the experienced leaders, trainers, and attack planners it was able to promote in previous years. It is focused on its security and survival at the expense of operations against the Homeland.

Al-Qa'ida's leadership in Pakistan continues efforts to inspire and guide some of its regional nodes, allies, and like-minded extremists to engage in terrorism against the West, but also stresses the importance of regional agendas and winning hearts and minds.  Absent the death of Ayman al-Zawahiri, Pakistan-based al-Qa'ida will retain its role as the ideological leader of the global jihad.

**Al-Qa'ida in the Arabian Peninsula (AQAP):**  From its base of operations in Yemen, the group remains resolute in targeting the Homeland, as well as U.S. and Western interests in Yemen and the Arabian Peninsula. However, ongoing counterterrorism pressure is likely slowing and/or delaying some attack plans. AQAP's recent attacks against Yemeni military targets highlight the group's ability to conduct complex attacks.

**Al-Qa'ida in Iraq (AQI), also known as the Islamic State of Iraq and Levant (ISIL):**  AQI/ISIL probably will attempt to take territory in Iraq and Syria to exhibit its strength in 2014, as demonstrated recently in Ramadi and Fallujah, and the group's ability to concurrently maintain multiple safe havens in Syria. However, its ability to hold territory will depend on the group's resources, local support, as well as the responses of ISF and other opposition groups in Syria.  While most Sunnis probably remain opposed to AQI's ideology and presence in Iraq and Syria, some Sunni tribes and insurgent groups appear willing to work tactically with AQI as they share common anti-government goals.  Baghdad's refusal to address long-standing Sunni grievances, and continued heavy-handed approach to counter-terror operations have led some Sunni tribes in Anbar to be more permissive of AQI's presence. Since the departure of U.S. forces at the end of 2011, AQI/ISIL has exploited the permissive security environment to increase its operations and presence in many locations and also has expanded into Syria and Lebanon to inflame tensions throughout the region. For example, AQI/ISIL claimed credit for the 2 January 2014 car bombing in Beirut, in a Hezbollah stronghold, furthering sectarian conflict and demonstrating its strength throughout the region.  And, the likelihood of more attacks in Lebanon is high. Concurrently, AQI remains in control of numerous Syrian cites such as Raqqah, Al-Bab, and Jarablus.

**Al-Nusrah Front:** The group is working to overthrow President Bashar al-Assad's regime by attacking the regime and its allies in Syria while building popular support through humanitarian aid campaigns. We judge al-Nusrah Front is seeking to expand its influence in the region and to advance its long-term goals of attacking Israel and strengthening the al-Qa'ida footprint in the Levant.

**Al-Qa'ida in the Lands of the Islamic Maghreb (AQIM):** Although counterterrorism pressure is probably compelling AQIM to consider alternative safehavens in other undergoverned areas in the region, the group most likely retains the capability to launch attacks against regional and Western interests in Mali and neighboring countries. During the next year, we expect AQIM to likely bolster its ties to al-Qa'ida-aligned terrorist groups in North and West Africa.

**Al-Shabaab:** The group continued to pose a threat to Western interests in East Africa as demonstrated by the September attack on the Westgate Mall in Nairobi, Kenya, which left at least 67 dead. During 2014, a regrouped al-Shabaab will continue to pose a threat to the fragile Somali government and its regional backers. It will attempt to replicate the success of its Westgate attack with additional operations outside Somalia.

## OTHER TERRORIST ACTIVITIES OF CONCERN

**Al-Murabitun:** This newly formed group poses a growing threat to Western interests in North Africa, based on the network's record of sophisticated attacks against Western mineral and energy interests in Niger and Algeria in 2013.

**Islamic Revolutionary Guard Corps–Qods Force (IRGC-QF) and Hizballah:** Iran continues to support and arm terrorist and militant groups in the Middle East. The IRGC–QF has supported pro-regime fighters in Syria, including elements from Lebanese Hizballah, Iraqi Shia groups, and Syrian militias. Captured video footage suggests the Qods Force is operating artillery and leading attacks against Syrian opposition. Hizballah also continues to send operatives to other locations outside Syria to plan external attacks and operations.

**Lashkar-e Tayyiba (LT):** The group has focused on India, but has dedicated greater operational resources from Indian Kashmir to Afghanistan in the years following the 2008 Mumbai attacks. LT ideologically advocates killing Americans and other Westerners, and in previous years has advanced plots ultimately disrupted by counterterrorism authorities in Australia and Denmark.

**Islamic Movement of Uzbekistan and the Islamic Jihad Union:** As Coalition forces withdraw from Afghanistan in 2014, these terrorist groups with Central Asian links might seize the opportunity to redirect some targeting efforts against Central Asia.

**Imirat Kavkaz (IK):** This North Caucasus-based terrorist group or IK–linked Caucasus–based militants were likely responsible for the October and December 2013 suicide attacks in Volgograd, Russia. These attacks and the July 2013 statement by IK leader Doku Umarov threatening the 2014 Winter Olympics suggests the likelihood of continued Islamic extremist attacks in Russia in this year aimed at undermining Moscow and deterring attendance at the February Winter Games in Sochi, Russia.

**Revolutionary Armed Forces of Colombia (FARC):** This group poses a significant and continuing threat to U.S. personnel and interests in 2014, despite peace talks with Bogota.

**European Home Grown Violent Extremists (HVEs):** Individuals will remain an ongoing security concern and challenge for Western security services as they radicalize within their home base; return home after gaining terrorist training and/or, combat experience abroad; or develop contacts domestically or abroad to plan attacks against Western interests. Although not all returning fighters will pose a threat, DIA is particularly concerned about self-initiated or "lone wolf" attacks on U.S. military and allied military members in Europe. The Revolutionary People's Liberation Party/Front (DHKP/C) also signaled a renewed effort to target U.S./DoD interests with its 1 February 2013 attack on the U.S. Embassy in Ankara and has proven resilient despite crackdowns on the organization in Turkey and elsewhere.

**U.S. Homegrown Violent Extremists (HVEs) and Insider Threats:** HVEs continue to pose the most likely terrorist threat to DoD, as evidenced by several successful attacks and numerous disrupted plots targeting DoD facilities, installations, and personnel in recent years. While they are less likely to generate complex and spectacular attacks than transnational terror groups, HVEs can conduct attacks with little or no warning, complicating efforts by law enforcement and intelligence agencies to detect and disrupt them. Since 2009, a small number of individuals working for or with access to DoD personnel and facilities have acted on behalf of or have been inspired by terrorist groups. We anticipate terrorist groups and sympathetic violent extremists will continue seek to establish relationships with individuals associated with DoD to collect information and conduct attacks.

## WEAPONS OF MASS DESTRUCTION (WMD) , DELIVERY SYSTEMS, PROLIFERATION, AND ADVANCED CONVENTIONAL WEAPONS

The proliferation and potential for use of WMD and ballistic missiles is a grave and enduring threat. Securing nuclear weapons and materials is a worldwide imperative to prevent accidents and the potential diversion of fissile or radiological materials. As technology proliferates chemical and biological weapons are becoming more sophisticated. Al-Qa'ida and some of its affiliate organizations aspire to acquire and employ chemical, biological, radiological and nuclear (CBRN) materials. They are most likely seeking low-level CBR agents, such as ricin, botulinum toxin, radiological dispersal devices, and toxic industrial chemicals like cyanide and chlorine as low cost alternatives.

We are concerned about the potential for terrorists to acquire Syrian WMD materials. While Syria's chemical and biological weapons stockpiles are currently under the control of the regime, al-Qa'ida and its regional affiliates could seek to obtain Syrian stockpiles should security be insufficient. We anticipate the movement of convoys carrying CW from its current locations for disposal could provide an opportunity for one or more of these groups to try to obtain CW agents or material.

Determined groups and individuals, as well as the proliferation networks they tie into, often work to sidestep international detection and avoid export-controls. Such entities regularly change the names of their front companies, operate in countries with permissive environments or lax enforcement, and avoid international financial institutions. Another military issue is the proliferation of advanced conventional weapons, especially air defense systems and anti-ship cruise missiles. We remain concerned especially with Russia's exports of these arms, including the SA-17, SA-22 and SA-20 surface-to-air missile (SAM) systems, as well as the supersonic Yakhont anti-ship cruise missile. Russia has exported several of these systems to countries of concern, including the SA-17 to Venezuela, and the SA-17, SA-22 and Yakhont to Syria. Iran continues to press Russia to sell it the SA-20, a modern long-range SAM. The 300–km range Yakhont poses a major threat to naval operations particularly in the eastern Mediterranean. Russia continues to market the Club-K cruise missile system, a family of weapons deployed inside standardized commercial shipping containers similar to those found on merchant vessels, freight rail trains, and road vehicles. The covert nature of this weapon would render identifying threat platforms very difficult and reduce warning of an attack.

China is expanding as a supplier of advanced conventional weapons, supplementing its traditional exports of basic battlefield equipment such as small arms, artillery and armored vehicles to include more advanced examples of long-range multiple launch rocket artillery, improved surface to air missile systems and anti-ship cruise missiles, and unmanned aerial vehicles, several of which are armed variants. China's rapid development of new products, aggressive marketing, and relatively low pricing will allow more countries with limited access to advanced weapons to acquire some of these capabilities.

## THEATER BALLISTIC MISSILES

Ballistic missiles are becoming more survivable, reliable, and accurate at greater ranges. Potential adversaries are basing more missiles on mobile platforms at sea and on land. Technical and operational measures to defeat missile defenses also are increasing. China, Iran, and North Korea, for example, exercise near simultaneous salvo firings from multiple locations to saturate missile defenses. Countries are designing missiles to launch from multiple transporters against a broad array of targets, enhancing their mobility and effectiveness on the battlefield. Shorter launch-preparation times and smaller footprints are making new systems more survivable, and many have measures to defeat missile defenses.

## SPACE AND COUNTERSPACE

Space is becoming an increasingly congested, competitive, and contested environment. The quantity and quality of foreign satellites on orbit is rapidly increasing and foreign countries are developing counters to the US space advantage, including methods to disrupt or deny access to communications; position, navigation, and timing; and intelligence, surveillance, and reconnaissance satellites.

**China:** Beijing is pursuing space efforts for military, economic and political objectives. China's military operates satellites for communications, navigation, earth resources, weather, intelligence, surveillance, and reconnaissance purposes, in addition to manned space and space exploration missions. Typically, China has emphasized the domestic and international benefits of its space program. Internationally, China views the success of these capabilities as a contributor to its growing status and influence, but refrains from highlighting any specific military applicability.

Regarding its counterspace activities, China's test of a ground-based anti-satellite missile in 2007 and the resulting debris generation in the atmosphere has been well publicized. If deployed, such a capability and the resultant orbital debris is a threat to all countries' military, civilian, and commercial space assets to the peaceful usage of outer space. Non-kinetic counterspace solutions in development also include jammers.

**Russia:** Moscow recognizes the strategic value of space, and understands space as a force multiplier and views US dependency on space for projection of military power as a vulnerability. Russia's space sector has experienced a series of failures in recent years but is taking steps to correct quality control problems within its satellite and space launch vehicle industries. In the past year, Russia completed population of its GLONASS navigation satellite constellation and is making gradual improvements to its communications, ballistic missile launch detection, and intelligence-gathering satellites. The Russian military has a highly advanced space surveillance network, a prerequisite for counterspace operations, and is modernizing and expanding these systems. Russia has satellite jamming capabilities and is pursuing other counterspace capabilities.

## HARD, DEEP, BURIED TARGETS/UNDERGROUND FACILITIES

The use of underground facilities (UGFs) to conceal and protect critical military and other assets and functions is widespread and expanding. UGFs conceal and increase the survivability of weapons of mass destruction, strategic command and control, leadership protection and relocation, military research and development, military production and strategic military assets. A significant trend of concern is the basing of ballistic and cruise missiles and other systems designed for anti-access/area denial weapons directly within UGFs. In addition, Russia, China, Iran, and North Korea operate national-level military denial and deception programs. These four states are devoting increased resources, and particular attention, to improving the denial and deception tactics, techniques, and procedures, for their road-mobile missile and cruise missile forces.

## REGIONAL THREATS

### MIDDLE EAST AND NORTH AFRICA

**Egypt:** The unrest following the July deposal of Mursi has been dealt with by the interim government through laws and tactics to quell dissent, sometimes violently. While the interim government promised an ambitious timetable for transition to an elected government, it has missed some of its own set deadlines. Countrywide protests by opposition groups have been overshadowed by terrorist violence, which is no longer limited to the Sinai. Growing popular opposition against military dominance in society threatens the cohesion of the political parties currently supporting the interim government. Frustration among Islamist political groups over changes to the constitution and their expulsion from political life and parts of civil society threatens to lead to radicalization. The new constitution was finalized by popular referendum with 98% approval and 38.6% participation, helped in part by changes to regulations to allow for easier voting, lack of free and fair environment in the run up to the elections, and the Muslim Brotherhood and majority of other opposition groups boycotting the vote. Cairo plans to begin the presidential election process in the spring and the parliamentary process in the summer.

Security in the Sinai Peninsula is particularly poor despite Egyptian security efforts there since fall of last year and domestic security elsewhere remains difficult. Increasingly lethal and brazen attacks on security and military forces in the Sinai persist even in areas garrisoned by large numbers of Egyptian forces.  Terrorist networks retain their capabilities and are demonstrating their resilience despite increased Egyptian CT efforts, while exploiting security vacuums in parts of the Sinai.

Security forces elsewhere in Egypt face frequent public disobedience, as anti-interim government Islamists focus on low-level resistance, such as student disturbances at university campuses, and avoid other forms of popular protest likely to be forcibly broken up by authorities.


**Syria:**  Three years into the conflict, Syria remains divided and neither the regime nor the opposition has a decisive advantage on the battlefield. The regime dominates central and western areas while the opposition remains dominant in northern and eastern areas. In late 2013, the regime acceded to the Chemical Weapons Convention (CWC) and began dismantling its chemical weapons program. The first shipment of CW components left Syria in January and the Organization for the Prevention of Chemical Weapons (OPCW) is supporting the ongoing removal.

Assad's inner circle and the Syrian military remain cohesive, but the military is stretched thin by constant operations. The regime's strategy has been to encircle the villages and suburbs surrounding opposition-held areas, and then employ artillery bombardments and air strikes before conducting clearing operations. Although these tactics are not new, the regime has demonstrated an increased proficiency and professionalism in their execution compared to the past and has relied more on irregular troops such as militias and Hizballah fighters. This increased effectiveness probably is at least in part due to Iranian support, particularly in training, advising, and intelligence. Syria continues to rely on Russia for major maintenance and refitting of its helicopters and likely other heavy equipment after 2 years of heavy use.

Hizballah continues to provide training, advice, and extensive logistic support to the Syrian government and its supporters. Hizballah has directly trained Syrian government personnel inside Syria and has facilitated IRGC–QF training of some Syrian forces. Hizballah also has contributed troops to Syrian regime offensives, playing a substantial combat role in operations in Damascus, al-Qusayr, Qalamoun, and other areas within Syria. Iran also has actively supported the Syrian regime in its fight against the opposition.

The Syrian regime maintains the military advantage – particularly in firepower and air superiority, but struggles with an overall inability to decisively defeat the opposition. The opposition has thus far failed to translate their tactical gains in the rural areas of northern and eastern Syria into gains in southern or western Syria. Competition over resources and violent infighting has limited the opposition's overall combat effectiveness. Ineffective distribution systems, weapons hoarding, and lack of a coherent and unified campaign plan has limited opposition success. Salafist and extremist groups are increasingly challenging Western-–backed elements such as the Syrian Military Council (SMC). The competition between groups, and sometimes violence, distracts them from their fight against the regime.

Syria's most prominent external political opposition group, the Syrian Opposition Coalition (SOC), struggles to gain internal legitimacy, and no group has been able to unite the diverse groups behind a strategy for replacing the regime. Saudi Arabia and Qatar are funding and arming Syrian rebels seeking to overthrow the Assad regime to weaken Iranian influence in the region and set the stage for a post-Assad government friendly to their own interests. Saudi Arabia worries about empowered jihadists in Syria while Qatar supports some Islamist groups.

Prior to its accession to the CWC, we believe Syria maintained an advanced CW program and had a stockpile that included either complete or binary components of mustard, sarin, and VX along with weapons systems to deliver these agents. Syria has signed, but did not ratify the Biological Weapons (BW) Convention. Syria may be capable of limited agent production, however we do not believe Syria has achieved a capability to use biological agents as effective mass-casualty weapons. We remain concerned about insurgents and terrorists attempting to acquire state WMD materials should security fail at CW sites in the wake of unrest or during movement to the coast. While Syria's chemical weapons stockpiles are currently under the control of the Syrian regime, Sunni terrorist groups including al-Qa'ida in Iraq/Islamic State of Iraq and the Levant (AQI/ISIL) and al-Nusrah Front have aspired to obtain WMD in the past.

Syria has several hundred SCUD-B, -C, and -D, and SS-21 SRBMs. Syria also has a domestic version of the Iranian Fateh-110 SRBM. All of Syria's missiles are mobile and can reach much of Israel and large portions of Iraq, Jordan, and Turkey from launch sites well within the country. Damascus relies on foreign help, mainly from Iran, to advance its solid-propellant rocket and missile development and production capability. Syria's liquid-propellant missile program also remains dependent on essential foreign equipment and assistance.

**Iran:** Tehran poses a major threat to U.S. interests through its regional ambitions, support to terrorist and militant groups, improving military capabilities and nuclear ambitions. Iran is active throughout the region and has increased its influence during the past twelve months in Syria, Iraq, Yemen, and Bahrain.

However, Iran has somewhat tempered its belligerent rhetoric since President Hasan Ruhani took office in August 2013. Ruhani's international message of moderation and pragmatism is intended to support Tehran's enduring objectives, which are to preserve the Supreme Leader's rule, counter Western influence, and establish Iran as the dominant regional power. Supreme Leader Ali Khamenei continues to dominate Iran's power structure as both the political-spiritual guide and the commander in chief of the armed forces.

Iran has threatened to temporarily impede international ship traffic transiting through the Strait of Hormuz if it is attacked or in response to further sanctions on its oil exports. Additionally, Iran has threatened to launch missiles against U.S. targets and our regional allies in response to an attack. Tehran could also employ its terrorist surrogates. However, it is unlikely to initiate or intentionally provoke a conflict or launch a preemptive attack.

In Iraq, Iran works closely with Baghdad to maintain its influence and its access to Syria and Levant via air and ground transport. Iran continues to fund, train, and support Iraqi Shia groups to defend the Shia-led government against the perceived threat of Sunni violence, including spillover from the conflict in Syria. Iran will likely use its leverage with Shia groups and Iraqi government officials to influence the 2014 Iraqi elections to maintain an Iran-friendly government regime in Baghdad.

In addition to its support of irregular forces, Iran is steadily improving its military capabilities. The navy is developing faster, more lethal surface vessels, growing its submarine force, expanding its cruise missile defense capabilities, and increasing its presence in international waters. The navy conducted its farthest out-of-area deployment to date in March 2013, docking in China, and for the first time ever an Iranian submarine visited India in December 2013. The navy aspires to travel as far as the Atlantic Ocean.

Iran is laboring to modernize its air and air defense forces under the weight of international sanctions. Each year, Iran unveils what it claims are state-of-the-art, Iranian-made systems, including SAMs, radars, unmanned aerial vehicles, and it did so again in 2013. It continues to seek an advanced long-range surface-to-air missile system.

Iran can strike targets throughout the region and into Eastern Europe. In addition to its growing missile and rocket inventories, Iran is seeking to enhance lethality and effectiveness of existing systems with improvements in accuracy and warhead designs. Iran is developing the Khalij Fars, an anti-ship ballistic missile which could threaten maritime activity throughout the Persian Gulf and Strait of Hormuz. Iran's Simorgh space launch vehicle shows the country's intent to develop intercontinental ballistic missile (ICBM) technology.

**Iraq:** Since the withdrawal of U.S. forces in December 2011, the Iraqi Security Forces (ISF) have struggled to secure all of Iraq, maintaining security primarily in Shia majority areas. Tensions between Sunnis and Shia, and Arabs and Kurds, have persisted due to the government's unwillingness to share power and the spill-over effects from the crisis in Syria. Violence levels are rising and likely will continue in 2014 as long as the Shia-dominated government avoids political accommodation and the conflict in Syria continues.

Iraqi Shia militant groups have largely refrained from attacks on U.S. interests and so far have initiated only limited operations against Sunni targets, despite rising AQI violence against Iraqi Shia and increasing demands for Shia militias to protect their communities. Shia militant groups have focused on building their popular base ahead of Iraq's 2014 national elections. They also continue to send fighters to Syria to augment Iranian-led, pro-regime forces and have conducted attacks against the Mujahedin-e Khalq (MEK) presence in Iraq. Despite their restraint in Iraq, Shia militants remain capable of violent action and they are preparing for violence to spill over from Syria.

The Iraqi Sunni population is increasingly distraught over its fortunes in Iraq. The government's refusal to reform de-Baathification and anti-terror laws—a key Sunni demand—deepens Sunni alienation. Anti-government demonstrations in Iraq's three major Sunni provinces have continued for a year. Recent violence in Ramadi and Fallujah in eastern Anbar Province sparked from Sunni perceptions that the Iraqi government aggressively targeted Sunni civilians. The situation in both cities is fluid and control of different portions of the cities and their surrounding areas will likely change. Unilateral Iraqi military action to contain the violence, if conducted by predominantly Shia units, would only deepen the divide and could convince Sunnis to reject future participation in the government.

ISF have been unable to stem rising violence in part because they lack mature intelligence, logistics, and other capabilities, and still require substantial assistance to integrate newly-acquired equipment. ISF have demonstrated the ability to put forces on the street, conduct static security of high-profile sites and events, and to operate checkpoints. However, these abilities have not enabled them to suppress AQI or other internal threats. ISF are increasingly challenged in Sunni majority and ethnically mixed areas of Iraq, especially Anbar and Ninewa Provinces. Iraqi military and police forces lack cohesion, are undermanned, and are poorly trained, equipped, and supplied. This leaves them vulnerable to terrorist attack, infiltration, and corruption.

The ISF is inadequately prepared to defend against external threats by land, air, or sea. Iraq's ground forces have limited ability to conduct and sustain conventional military operations against a peer, and Iraq has few forces and capabilities to defend its airspace or coastal waters. Iraq has pursued numerous foreign military sales contracts to overcome equipment shortfalls and gaps in ISF capabilities. Iraq is diversifying its defense acquisitions with more Russian and other non-U.S. equipment. In November 2013, Iraq received an initial delivery of attack helicopters from arms deals with Russia worth over $4 billion that include air defense systems and other arms. The United States also completed delivery of C-130J transport aircraft and 30 armed reconnaissance helicopters in May 2013. In December 2013 Iraq concluded a $2.1 Billion deal with South Korea for FA-50 combat-capable training aircraft. However, we expect it will take several years for Iraqi military strength and capabilities to improve substantially.

**Yemen:** The security situation throughout Yemen remains tenuous, with government security forces focused either on providing security in Sanaa or working to counter AQAP. Iranian meddling in Yemen's domestic affairs, to include support to some armed Huthi groups in the North and some secessionists in the South, presents an additional security risk. Apolitical transition process, including efforts to reform the military, is ongoing but proceeding slowing. The National Dialogue Conference concluded in January, allowing forward movement on preparations for constitutional reform and national elections. Notwithstanding political progress, Yemen's failing economy, dwindling water resources, and food insecurity will further complicate efforts.

**Libya:** Militias that won the revolution against the Qadhafi regime are now also threatening both the transition process and overall security. Militias present a challenge to internal stability despite Tripoli's recent progress integrating some armed groups into its security forces. To counteract the militias' power, Tripoli seeks international assistance to establish a General Purpose Force (GPF) and controlled security entity. Militias loyal to Federalists factions, Berbers, and other minority groups have also occupied oil facilities, decreasing Libya's oil production from 1.4 million barrels per day to 250,000, and costing the Libyan government over $7.5 billion in revenues.

Mid-November 2013 incidents in Tripoli, Benghazi, and Darnah resulted in more than 40 civilian deaths. Public and government backlash forced militias to withdraw from these cities. These militia elements have withdrawn but have not disarmed, and will likely attempt to return to urban areas after pressure recedes. Other militias not involved in the incidents also remain. Heavily armed militias will likely continue to threaten stability over the next year. GPF will not be capable of restoring security or central government authority for at least one-to-two years.

## SOUTH ASIA

**Pakistan:** The new government elected in May 2013 seeks to rebuild relations with the United States, including the resumption of the strategic dialogue process. Relations have improved, but anti-U.S. sentiment and criticism of Pakistan's cooperation with the U.S. among the population remains high.

In 2013, the civilian government, Army, and the Supreme Court all transitioned to new leadership, which were the first leadership changes for these institutions in nearly five years. Nawaz Sharif was elected for his third-term as Prime Minister after his party won a simple majority in the May elections. Gen Raheel Sharif (no relation) was appointed Pakistan's Chief of Army Staff following the retirement of Gen (ret) Ashfaq Parvez Kayani in late November 2013. Justice Tassaduq Hussain Jillani became the Chief Justice of Pakistan's Supreme Court in December, replacing Iftikhar Muhammad Chaudhry who retired due to age. Jillani will only hold the position for seven months and the media speculates he will be less of an activist than his predecessor.

The civilian government is focused on addressing Pakistan's pressing economic issues as well as coordinating a counterterrorism strategy. However, its pursuit of treason charges against former President/Chief of Army Staff Musharraf risks civil-military tension as the case proceeds because it could tarnish the image of the Army and put other senior officers in jeopardy of prosecution.

Approximately one-third of Pakistan's army and paramilitary forces are deployed in the Federally Administered Tribal Areas (FATA) and Khyber Pakhtunkhwa Province (KPP) to support combat operations at any given time. Over the past year, Pakistan conducted counterinsurgency operations targeting militants in the FATA and KPP which directly threaten Pakistan's internal security. Despite some success disrupting Pakistan-focused militant activity, Pakistan's counterinsurgency efforts continue to struggle. The Pakistan military has been engaged in some limited security operations in North Waziristan, although it is unclear when large scale operations will commence.

Tension with Kabul increased after Afghan and Pakistani military forces exchanged direct fire across the border in May 2013. However, the election of a new Pakistani government has provided an opportunity for Islamabad to re-engage with Kabul in an effort to improve border cooperation and cross-border trade in line with the new government's focus on improving Pakistan's economy. Pakistan continues to release Taliban prisoners and has sought ways to support the Afghan peace process. However, long-standing issues including periodic cross-border shelling and the presence of militants on both sides of the border continue to foment distrust and impede broader cooperation.

Prime Minister Sharif has publically emphasized his desire to improve relations with India since assuming office in June 2013. Several high profile meetings, including the first meeting between the Pakistani and Indian Directors General of Military Operations in 14 years, generated commitments to further dialogue. However, tensions over the Line of Control in Kashmir, delays in the prosecution of the alleged Mumbai attack planners in Pakistan, and domestic political constraints in both capitals will continue to hinder progress this year. A major terrorist attack against India linked to Pakistan would nullify prospects for improved relations and could escalate tensions.

**India:** In 2013, India continued its efforts to maintain its economic and military ties with important regional partners in East and Southeast Asia. India and Japan conducted their second bilateral naval exercise in the Bay of Bengal in December, and India and Vietnam increased their naval engagement in November. India also signed a trilateral agreement with the Maldives and Sri Lanka in 2013 aimed at improving maritime security cooperation.

New Delhi and Beijing continue to conduct military-to-military engagement and discuss their longstanding border dispute. The two countries signed a Border Defense Cooperation Agreement in October 2013 to reinforce existing procedures to prevent standoffs along their disputed border from escalating. The Indian Army and People's Liberation Army also resumed ground exercises, conducting a counter-terrorism exercise in China during November, the first since 2008.

India seeks a moderate government in Afghanistan that will deny anti-Indian militant groups the use of its territory from which to launch attacks on India . New Delhi has pledged economic and development assistance and provides training to Afghan National Security Force personnel at military institutions in India. Indian and Afghan Special Forces conducted their first combined exercise in India in late December.

India is in the midst of a major military modernization effort – undertaken by all three military services – to address problems with its aging equipment and to posture itself to defend against both Pakistan and China. Major acquisitions that occurred in 2013 included the delivery of a Russian-built aircraft carrier, a Talwar Class Frigate, additional Su-30MKI FLANKERs, U.S. built C-17s and P-8I maritime patrol aircraft, and the commissioning of India's indigenously-built nuclear-powered ballistic missile submarine. Military modernization is progressing slowly, however, because of India's cumbersome procurement process, budget constraints, and a domestic defense industry that struggles to provide military equipment that meets service requirements.

## AFRICA

Africa faces a myriad of security challenges that will require continued U.S. attention.

**Somalia:** Somalia saw limited progress on its political and security fronts in 2013, as internal divisions hobbled the new government's development and international forces reached the limit of their ability to hold territory. Al-Shabaab having lost control of major cities, and the federal government made steps toward regional integration. Despite significant and public internal divisions in 2013, al-Shabaab continued to conduct attacks, often complex in nature, targeting AMISOM, Somali government, and international targets in Somalia. Al-Shabaab-affiliated militants also continued to carry out attacks in Kenya, most prominently the late September attack on the Westgate Mall in Nairobi. Kenya. The recent authorization of additional troops for the African Union (AU) force will permit the resumption of offensive action against al-Shabaab in 2014, and the government will need to capitalize on these security gains. On a positive note, security measures adopted by international shipping companies, coupled with international naval patrols, have helped reduce piracy off the Horn of Africa to its lowest levels in five years; no vessels were hijacked in 2013. Within the Africa Horn region in Djibouti, where DoD has its largest footprint on the continent, there is concern regarding the increasing presence of foreign countries' activities.

**Central African Republic:** A spike in violence in December 2013 in the Central African Republic prompted the expeditious deployment of international peacekeepers, who will struggle to secure the entire country in the absence of a reliable host nation security force. While the U.S. is not engaged in combat in the CAR, U.S. logistics operations in support of French and African Union forces also face potential threats. Despite the elimination of the M23 armed group in late 2013 in eastern Democratic Republic of the Congo, continued military operations alone will not solve the long-standing underlying causes of conflict, such as poverty, human rights violations, and the lack of government control. Moreover, the presence of Rwandan rebels whose leaders are dedicated to the overthrow of the Rwandan government, probably will remain a destabilizing factor over the next year at least. Five years of sustained pursuit by Uganda's military has reduced the Lord's Resistance Army's numbers and forced them to split up into smaller groups; however, the group still conducts hit-and-run resupply attacks on civilians.

**Nigeria:** Domestic instability, most notably from the terrorist group Boko Haram in the northeast, is a concern. Abuja's offensive operations in 2013 against Boko Haram were initially successful in lowering the number of attacks, but, by September, the group had expanded its attack campaign and now conducts high-casualty attacks on a near-daily basis. Because Abuja is focusing its security services on a number of internal operations, its military is overstretched, eroding its ability to support external peacekeeping missions. Moreover, maritime crime increased significantly in the Gulf of Guinea in 2013, surpassing the number of attacks off the coast of Somalia for the first time since 2008. Criminal networks have expanded their range of operations and become adaptable and sophisticated, while regional states lack the maritime security capacity to secure shared waters, largely due to a lack of political will, equipment, maintenance capacity, training, and cooperation.

# EAST ASIA

**China:** The People's Liberation Army (PLA) is building a modern military capable of achieving success on a 21$^{st}$ century battlefield. The PLA is developing capabilities to protect China's defined territorial integrity, which includes Taiwan and other land and maritime claims along around China's periphery, preserve China's political system and ensure sustainable economic and social development. Preparation for a Taiwan conflict with U.S. intervention remains the primary driver of the PLA's evolving force structure, weapons development, operational planning and training.

China has spent as much as $240 billion on military–related goods and services in 2013, in contrast to the $119.5 billion Beijing reported in its official military budget. This budget omits major categories, but it does show spending increases for domestic military production and programs to improve professionalism and the quality of life for military personnel.

Disputed territorial claims in the East and South China Seas remain potential flashpoints. The Chinese announcement in November 2013 that it was establishing an air identification zone (ADIZ) over portions of the East China Sea has increased tensions since this ADIZ overlaps with other preexisting ADIZ's and covers territory administrated by Japan and the Republic of Korea. China's announcement raised tensions and increased the risk of incidents that could undermine peace, security, and prosperity in the region.

China's ground force is seeking to restructure itself into a mechanized, modular force that can conduct joint operations anywhere along China's borders. This effort is currently taking shape with an emphasis on building and outfitting brigades as the main operational unit and creating flexible special operations forces, improved army aviation units, and C2 capabilities with improved networks providing real-time data transmissions within and between units

China's air force is transforming from a force oriented solely on territorial defense into one capable of both offshore offensive and defensive roles – including strike, air and missile defense, early warning, and reconnaissance. It is also seeking to improve its strategic projection by increasing its long-range transport and logistical capabilities. Modernization efforts include investing in stealth technology. China also continues negotiations with Russia for Su-35 fighter aircraft; however, a contract is unlikely to be signed until later this year, at the earliest.

The PLA navy is developing the JIN-class nuclear-powered ballistic missile submarine and JL-2 submarine-launched ballistic missile. We expect the navy will make their first nuclear deterrence patrols in 2014. It has also recently deployed for the first time a nuclear-powered attack submarine to the Indian Ocean. China is also continuing negotiations for the joint-design and production for a new advanced conventional submarine based on the Russian LADA-class. China's investment in naval weapons primarily focuses on anti-air and anti-surface capabilities to achieve periodic and local sea and air superiority within the first island chain. China's first aircraft carrier, commissioned in late 2012, will not reach its full potential until it acquires an operational fixed-wing air regiment over the next several years.

To modernize its nuclear missile force, China is also adding more survivable road-mobile systems and enhancing its silo-based systems. This new generation of missiles is intended to ensure the viability of China's strategic deterrent by ensuring a second strike capability.

The military is also augmenting the over 1,200 conventional short-range ballistic missiles deployed opposite Taiwan with a limited but growing number of conventionally armed, medium-range ballistic missiles, including the DF-16, which will improve China's ability to strike regional targets. China also continues to deploy growing numbers of the DF-21D anti-ship ballistic missile.

**Democratic People's Republic of Korea's (DPRK):** Pyongyang's primary national objectives consist of preserving the current authority structure under the leadership of Kim Jong Un, improving the country's dysfunctional struggling economy, and deterring foreign adversaries from taking actions which could threaten the regime. In early 2013, Kim Jong Un articulated a policy of simultaneously pursuing the production of nuclear weapons and the development of the national economy. Pyongyang is likely to maintain this course for the foreseeable future.

Kim Jong Un continues to exercise his authority in both senior Party and military positions, including First Secretary of the Korea Workers' Party, Supreme Commander of the Korean Peoples' Army, and First Chairman of the National Defense Commission. Since becoming leader of North Korea, Kim Jong Un has replaced or reassigned a large number of many senior party and military officials, placing younger officials more closely associated with him in key assignments. Kim's execution of his powerful uncle Chang Song-taek in December 2013 eliminated the most influential senior Party official remaining from his father's era and sent a strong message to regime elites that the formation of factions or potential challenges to Kim Jong Un will not be tolerated.

After Chang's execution, Pyongyang reiterated threats to attack South Korea for what it calls interference in its internal affairs. Although North Korea's large, forward-positioned conventional forces are capable of launching an attack on South Korea, the North's military suffers from logistics shortages, largely outdated equipment, and inadequate training. Pyongyang likely knows that an attempt to reunify the Korean Peninsula by force would fail, and that any major attack on the South would trigger a robust counterattack. Recent conventional military improvements have focused on developing the North's defensive capabilities and ability to conduct limited-scale military provocations, especially near the demilitarized zone and along the disputed maritime boundary in the Yellow Sea.

The Korean People's Army conducts the majority of its training during the winter training cycle, from December through March. North Korea is stressing increased realism in military training, but training still appears to do little more than maintain basic competencies. Because of its conventional military deficiencies, North Korea also has concentrated on improving its deterrence capabilities, especially its nuclear technology and ballistic missile forces. The North conducted a nuclear test in February 2013, and in April announced its intention to 'adjust and alter' the use of its existing nuclear facilities, including the plutonium production reactor and uranium enrichment facility at Yongbyon.

On the nuclear front, we assess that North Korea has followed through on its announcement by expanding the size of its Yongbyon enrichment facility and restarting the reactor that was previously used for plutonium production. The regime is probably pursuing a uranium enrichment capability for nuclear weapons development, and the restart and operation of its plutonium production reactor could provide the North with additional plutonium for nuclear weapons. It also seeks to develop longer-range ballistic missiles capable of delivering nuclear weapons to the United States, and continues efforts to bring its KN08 road mobile ICBM, which it paraded in July 2013, to operational capacity. In December, 2012, the North also used its Taepo-Dong-2 launch vehicle to put a satellite in orbit, thus demonstrating its capabilities for a number of long-range missile applicable technologies.

## RUSSIA

Russia continues to actively pursue its active foreign and defense policies, both along its periphery and elsewhere. In 2014, we expect Moscow will continue efforts to expand its influence in Eurasia by pushing its neighbors to increase cooperation with Russia and Russian–led organizations rather than the West, as Moscow recently did with Ukraine and Armenia. Russian leaders likely regard their support of Syria as a success and Moscow will continue to promote a negotiated resolution to the crisis, consider higher-profile defensive arms deliveries on a case-by-case basis, block efforts to gain UN authorization for military intervention, and insist that the Syrians themselves rather than external forces must determine any transition in power. Russian leadership further views the recent P5+1 agreement an opportunity to enhance bilateral relations with Tehran, although they will be wary of improvement in relations between Iran and the United States and European Union. Russia is ready to exploit any deterioration of relations between the United States and its allies and will move to offer support to such states.

Russia's Afghanistan policy reflects an uneasy balance between Moscow's wish for stability in Afghanistan and its desire to prevent any long-term U.S. military presence in Central Asia. With the drawdown of U.S. forces this year, Russia is increasingly worried about security threats flowing from Afghanistan. Russia maintains friendly ties with the Afghan government, but only provides modest aid. However, Moscow views the Afghan National Security Forces as insufficiently trained to secure Afghanistan after the departure of ISAF forces in 2014. Russia believes that bordering Central Asian states will be vulnerable to a spillover of violence and expanded narcotics trafficking. Moscow probably wishes to seize upon the departure of coalition forces from Central Asia—most notably the forthcoming closure of the Manas Transit Center in Kyrgyzstan—to reassert its influence in the region, particularly in the security sphere.

Russia's ten-year rearmament plan is a top priority for the armed forces, but it faces funding and implementation risks owing in part to a potential decline in oil and gas revenues, spending inefficiencies, an aging industrial base, and corruption. Russia spent an announced $66 billion on its armed forces in 2013, and the current budget plan calls for a 12.9 percent inflation-adjusted increase in 2014.

We expect Russia's military modernization will lead to a more agile and compact force capable of more modern forms of warfare. A future force will be smaller, but more capable of handling a range of contingencies on Russia's periphery. We expect continued effort on improvement of joint operations capabilities and rearmament because of the high priority Russian leadership places on these portfolios. The general purpose forces will continue to acquire new equipment in the near-term, but deliveries will be small and largely consist of modernized Soviet-era weapons. Russia also has purchased select foreign systems, such as France's Mistral amphibious assault ship, unmanned aerial vehicles from Israel, and Italian light armored vehicles. The first Mistral, purchased from France, was launched in France on 15 October 2013.

Russia will continue to maintain a robust and capable arsenal of strategic and nonstrategic nuclear weapons for the foreseeable future. To support this policy, the Russian government is making strong investments in its nuclear weapon programs. Priorities for the strategic nuclear forces include force modernization and command and control facilities upgrades. Russia will field more road-mobile SS-27 Mod-2 ICBMs with multiple independently targetable reentry vehicles. It also will continue development of the RS-26 intercontinental ballistic missile, the *Dolgorukiy* ballistic missile submarine and SS-NX-32 Bulava submarine-launched ballistic missile, and next-generation cruise missiles.

## LATIN AMERICA

**Mexico**: President Enrique Pena Nieto will continue to prioritize reducing homicide, kidnapping and extortion rates as the central element of his security strategy. He will rely on large-scale military troop deployments to reduce high-profile violence involving drug trafficking organizations. The military remains the lead on these efforts as police professionalization progresses slowly. At the state and municipal levels, police face the challenges of ongoing elevated violence, corruption, limited budgets and lack of government oversight.

The Pena Nieto administration has had some security successes. In one year the military has fulfilled more than half of its high value targeting objectives for its six-year term, arresting or killing 71 drug traffickers of a list of 122 priority targets. Intentional homicides declined for the second consecutive year, continuing a trend which began under the previous administration, but reported kidnappings and extortion have increased. More recently, the Michoacán state government called on the federal government to address a growing conflict between vigilante or self-defense groups and traffickers, complicating the security picture for the administration, and potentially pulling resources from ongoing security operations elsewhere in the country.

Mexican cartels are expanding their presence throughout the Western Hemisphere and partner with other criminal groups in the region to transship and distribute cocaine. Mexico is already the principal transit country for U.S.-bound cocaine and the primary foreign supplier of methamphetamine, heroin, and marijuana to the United States. The networks of Mexico's nine principal drug trafficking organizations also extend to six of seven continents, with the Sinaloa Cartel and Los Zetas having the farthest reach into these lucrative international markets. In addition to trafficking and distributing drugs, Mexican traffickers rely on organized crime syndicates and small criminal groups to launder money, obtain precursor chemicals for drug production in Mexico, and in some cases, produce drugs on their behalf.

**Honduras, El Salvador and Guatemala:** The proliferation of drug trafficking groups and record-high violence will ensure these countries continue to employ the armed forces to combat drug trafficking and perform traditional law enforcement functions while ongoing police reforms attempt to bolster police capabilities. Guatemala also is plagued with drug traffickers throughout the country and has one of the highest murder rates in the world.

**Colombia:** The Defense Ministry is maintaining security operations against the FARC while Bogota conducts peace talks, which have become President Juan Manuel Santos's focus prior to the May 2014 presidential election. Santos replaced his defense high command in August 2013 and the Defense Ministry implemented a revised counterinsurgency strategy—Sword of Honor II—in October. While the revised campaign seeks to emphasize civil action programs, kinetic operations will continue under Sword of Honor II.

Colombia's counterdrug performance is the strongest in the region, and potential cocaine production has decreased in recent years, but the country remains the leading producer of U.S.-bound cocaine.

**Venezuela:** Economic stress continues to build in Venezuela with inflation of 56 percent in 2013 and scarcity of basic consumer goods, but frustration with President Nicolas Maduro's policies and the economy has not led to widespread sustained protests and the military leadership supports him.   High crime rates – some of the highest in the region – added an additional level of insecurity, requiring the deployment of law enforcement and military troops.  President Maduro lacks the charisma and popularity enjoyed by late President Hugo Chavez.  Historically, military support has been critical for any Venezuelan president's ability to maintain power and ensure stability, and Maduro has provided incentives to build military loyalty.  He has announced pay increases, and plans to improve military housing and health benefits.  The military continues to modernize and will receive additional Chinese and Russian equipment deliveries. Caracas took possession of two Chinese medium transport aircraft in November and Russian long-range surface-to-air missile systems in April 2013.  Caracas also increasingly employs the military in domestic roles.

**Cuba:** President Raul Castro will manage his nation's political, socioeconomic, and security force conditions to maintain regime viability and keep the likelihood of a mass migration to a minimum. While he will continue to implement economic reforms slowly and cautiously, Castro will adjust the pace as needed to assure his regime's continued grip on power. Cuban intelligence services, having proven very capable of penetrating key U.S. and DoD targets, remain the predominant counterintelligence threat to the U.S. emanating from Latin America.